Local Online Marketing

Small Business Online Advertising For Retail And Service Businesses

By Claude Whitacre

LocalProfitGeyser.com

If You Want Customers To Find You, The #1 Rule is; You Must Be Where The Buyers Are Looking.
If you own a local business, have you ever heard a customer say, "I Found You Online"? Do You Want To Hear That Far More Often?

Local Online Marketing was written specifically for the small business owner that has a retail store or service business serving their local area....and nobody else.

Do you own a small business and want to increase the number of customers you get from online advertising? Do you want more internet generated leads for your business? It's no longer enough to have a website and hope that people find you online. You have to be online. And you have to be online everywhere your customers are looking.

Take Back All The "Loyal" Customers You Have Lost To Online Pirates, And More

Discover How Just Ten Minutes A Day Will Get You The Following;
-Multiple page one Google search results for your local business.
-Online business listings that get you found On Google.
-Your website seen in multiple local Google searches.

-The best ways to get top Google Business Local listings
-How to quickly dominate YouTube search results..Make your videos go viral!
-How to use your competitor's advertising to bring real buyers to your business.
-How to beat your competition. Get your business found first in any online search
-The best types of YouTube videos to attract customers like a magnet.
-The proven ways to make your business easy to find for local online shoppers.

Why does it take only ten minutes a day? Because you won't be doing all the things that don't work.

You must be where your customers are looking for what you sell. And that's on the search engines like Google, Yahoo, and Bing. Online advertising is where you will get the best results, and at the lowest cost.

Invest just ten minutes a day following this guide, and you'll get everything you need to get your business seen online by local buyers. Use what you learn in this "Packed to the gills" manual, and you can hit the ground running.
Read the book, take notes, and let's get your business *noticed.*

CONTENTS

ACKNOWLEDGMENTS

I wrote the book myself. Hunter Miller assembled the chapters and helped with proofreading.

Amazon.com has a program called CreateSpace that makes publishing incredibly easy, and that's the method we used for this book.

My wife Cheryl helps in ways I can't even describe. She patiently listens to each new speech, technique, or training method. She gives me her opinion and her support.

I've made more than my share of mistakes in life. But in finding a great wife? I chose well.

And the fact that she feels the same way makes life so much more fun.

Read this first.

This book was specifically written for self-employed small business owners. Sure, the methods we discuss will work for larger companies, and the internet doesn't care if you are self-employed or not. But I'm writing this for you. Why?

Because I'm one of you. So I know how you think. Almost all self-employed business owners are independent, non-followers who make all their own decisions. Sound familiar?

Most of us are also woefully behind the times when it comes to all things online. Maybe that's why you bought this book. See, almost all of us are still selling the same way we were 20 years ago. The trouble is that our customers are buying *differently* than they were 5 years ago. The year 2009 was the first year that more business phone numbers were looked up online than in the print phone book or by dialing 411. More than twice as many people are looking online to find a supplier than there are people looking in the print Yellow Pages.

More clothing was sold last year online than was sold in retail stores or mail-order catalogs combined....

Are the hairs on the back of your neck standing up just a little?

It's more than just saying "The writing is on the wall". That blaring sound you hear? That's your customers blasting in your ears trying to wake you up to the way they want to buy!

You may be one of the many small business owners that think the internet is providing unfair competition. After all, anyone can find anything cheaper online than in a retail store, right?

Have you ever had a customer ask you questions only to buy online from a competitor?
We have *all* had that experience. It's time to turn the tables. How would you like the customers to gather information online, and then come to *you* to buy *locally*? It's an experience I have every day, as do all of my clients.

The internet is a super highway jammed with customers eager to learn about what you sell, and looking for the best place to buy it. This book is written with one major purpose... to show you how to become the "Go To Guy" that every local online search leads your buyers to seek out.

Fasten your seat belts.

Introduction

What you are getting here is the result of over two years of continual effort to use the internet promoting my own local business. In the beginning, there was lots of trial and error, too many dead ends, false starts, and much aggravation. Eventually I found methods that really work, techniques that really generate profit, and resources that make the job easier. The result is this book.

Like you, I own a small business. I know the frustrations that come with putting money into advertising and getting nothing back. Every advertising rep has a new promise of media that will make you rich. It seems every book on marketing for small business owners is written by someone who has *never owned* a business. I practice what I preach. Everything I show you, I'm using myself. Today.

I may as well get this out of the way. I have a prejudice. I don't like books on marketing written by people who have never done anything they teach. There are lots of books on local advertising and marketing that are written by consultants who have never spent a dime on advertising, never tested an advertising technique, and have never lost money when their ideas backfire. I do like reading business books by people who are actually doing business. If you are a self-employed business owner, large or small, you have my respect. My hat is off to you. We have much in common.

Everything I learned that I give you in this book, I learned the hard, slow, expensive way. I'm betting you know how that feels. So I'm not going to waste your time with theories and platitudes.

There are no parables or philosophy on how business *should* be run. Every example is true, every figure accurate. Everything I show you is tested, proven, and profitable. It works. If you want to use online marketing to promote your local business, you just hit the Mother Load.

Here is how this all came about.

Currently at the time I'm writing this, I own a retail store in Wooster Ohio, The Sweeper Store.
In the first 8 years, our retail business has increased an annual average of 81% a year. How I accomplished that is in my book **The Unfair Advantage Small Business Advertising Manual**. I did all this with virtually *no* local online marketing.

Then, in 2007 the economy crashed. It affected my business dramatically as I'm sure it did yours. I knew I needed a huge boost in business. Advertising online seemed like the best choice.

I was getting profitable results from my offline advertising, but local online marketing was a mystery to me. And since most customers now start the buying process online, I knew that's where the real business was going to come from.

My first attempts at local online promotion were clumsy. I used the popular method of *guessing* what would work. Maybe you can identify with that. We built a local retail store website. It hosted a couple of videos of product demonstrations, and brought in a few customers a month...customers ready to buy a high end vacuum cleaner. This happened every month, consistently, at almost no cost to me. Manna from Heaven.

We would have customers come in the store and say "We saw you online". The only promotion we were doing for our website was our website URL in our print Yellow Page listing and mentioning it in our print ads.

One day I looked on Google to find our listing. We were listed #9 in Google Maps. (Now Google Places) But we were not listed until page 5 of the Google search listings. If you were looking locally to buy what we sell, you were going to find tons of competitors before you were even going to see my listing.

So I decided to do something about it.

I bought over a dozen books on online marketing. I went to several seminars on the subject. I spent two years basically groping for ways to improve my online results. The books all covered the same material, The Gurus I listened to weren't telling me anything that I could put to use promoting my local small business. They were just repeating what was in the books. But I actually thought I was making progress. After all, I had a local retail website...it had videos on it...what more did I *need*?

My breakthrough came when I joined a group of very successful business owners that were meeting once a month to exchange marketing ideas.

We learned that there are things you can do to improve your Google Business listing position. But far more importantly, I learned how to dominate the local Google search results. I eventually learned how to make all local online roads lead to me and my business. This information is *Game Changing*.

I decided to invest all my spare time (when not working with customers at my store), promoting my business online. I *manually* submitted my business listing to over 240 Yellow Page and other local search directories. Within 30 days I was listed #1 in Google Places (Now Google Business). But I still wasn't anywhere to be found when a customer did a local search on the Google search engine.

So I went on a binge of writing content and submitting it to sites that posted my information. I posted videos, wrote articles, and manually submitted them everywhere I could find.

On the next page is a screen shot of the Google page one results for a local search "vacuum cleaners Wooster Ohio"

This is 30 days *after I submitted my content*, using the rest of the system you are going to be learning here.

The difference is *stark*.

The arrows to the right of the page are pointing to listings that are mine.

I dominate the entire first page of Google.

+Hunter Search Images Maps Play YouTube News Gmail Drive Calendar More ▾

Google   vacuum cleaners wooster ohio

Web   Images   Maps   Shopping   Videos   More ▾   Search tools

About 13,600 results (0.25 seconds)

Vacuum Cleaners Wooster Ohio|Vacuum Cleaner Repairs|Air Purifiers
sweeperstoreonline.com/
Shopping for **vacuum cleaners**, ceiling fans, heaters, or air purifiers? **Wooster Ohio**
shoppers buy their **vacuum cleaner** parts, HEPA filters, **vacuum cleaner** bags, ...

Vacuum Cleaners Wooster Ohio: Wooster OH Vacuum Cleaners ...
www.youtube.com/watch?v...
Jul 5, 2010 - 3 min - Uploaded by sweeperstore
http://www.sweeperstoreonline.com offers **vacuum cleaners**:
Both upright and canister vacuums. We also sell ...

Riccar Vibrance **Vacuum Cleaner Wooster OH**: Wooster Ohio Riccar ...
www.youtube.com/watch?v...
Jul 31, 2010 - 7 min - Uploaded by sweeperstore
http://www.vacuumcleanerswoosterohio44691.com. This Is The
Riccar Vibrance. The Riccar Is Our Most ...

Vacuum Cleaners Wooster OH| Wooster Ohio Vacuum Cleaner ...
www.youtube.com/watch?v=kf ...
Oct 24, 2010 - 2 min - Uploaded by sweeperstore
Which is better for you, and upright or canister **vacuum cleaner**?
Find out more about **vacuum cleaners** at ...

Vacuum Cleaners Wooster Ohio: Vacuum Cleaner History And Little ...
www.youtube.com/watch?v...
Sep 11, 2012 - 26 sec - Uploaded by vacuumcleanerwooster
Vacuum Cleaners Wooster Ohio: Vacuum Cleaner History And
Little Known Facts Family Pet Hair And Pet ...

Lightweight **Vacuum Cleaners Wooster OH** - YouTube
www.youtube.com/watch?v=-Oes ...
Jul 11, 2010 - 8 min - Uploaded by sweeperstore
http://www.sweeperstoreonline.com Part 2 to Riccar RSL4
Demonstration at The Sweeper Store in **Wooster** ...

More videos for **vacuum cleaners wooster ohio** »

Vacuum Cleaners Wooster Ohio - YouTube
www.youtube.com/user/sweeperstore
Vacuum cleaner buying tips, vacuum features, **vacuum cleaner** comparisons,
vacuum cleaner reviews.
▶ 1:35 Claude Whitacre on Local Small Business ...   Mar 6, 2011
▶ 0:31 Claude Whitacre Speaking In Chicago On Local ...   Mar 6, 2011

VacuumCleanersWoosterOhio |We Sell Vacuums, Parts, And More!
vacuumcleanerswoosterohio.com/
Shopping for **vacuum cleaners**, ceiling fans, heaters, or air purifiers? **Wooster Ohio**
shoppers buy their **vacuum cleaner** parts, HEPA filters, **vacuum cleaner** bags, ...

Rainbow **Vacuum Cleaner** Review From **Wooster Ohio** by Claude ...
www.articlecity.com/articles/gadgets_and.../article_2210.shtml
The Rainbow **vacuum cleaner** is the one that uses water to filter out the dust, pollen,
germs, dust mites, and smoke from your room. In our store in **Wooster Ohio**, ...

Vacuum Cleaners Repair & Service in **Wooster, OH** - AOL Local ...
yellowpages.aol.com/vacuum-cleaners-repair-and.../oh/wooste ...
5+ items - Find great **Vacuum Cleaners** Repair & Service in **Wooster, OH** ...
Duck's Sew & Vac   330-345-3825   1828 Cleveland Rd   **Wooster**
Watson's Discount **Vacuum**   419-289-2151   2175 Claremont Ave Ashland

Gooooooooogle ›
1 2 3 4 5 6 7 8 9 10   Next

Advanced search   Search Help   Give us feedback

Google Home   Advertising Programs   Business Solutions   Privacy & Terms
About Google

The changes to my search engine listing came fast. Within 30 days, my business information was listed #1 in the Google search engine results for the search term:

"Vacuum Cleaners Wooster Ohio" (the most popular local search phrase for my business).

It was also listed number *two*...and *three....all the way up to number eight*! I also had five videos on the first page of the local Google search.

This result is for the *same* search phrase, the *same* area, the *same* search engine.....Just 30 days later.

Side note: I can't wait until you read this book. I have to tell you this now. One of the huge benefits of dominating page one of a Google search...is that you crowd out your competitors, *sometimes all of them*. I can't promise this will happen for you, but I have lots of letters from clients that tell me it happened for *them*.

My business improved dramatically. I track what causes people to come in the store and buy from us. We ask them at the checkout counter. The number of people that said "I found you online", "I read your information online" and "I saw your video online" multiplied. This online activity is generating many thousands of dollars more in profits every month. Within 90 days of posting these listings on Google, our business, generated from online sources, increased by 407%. I can't guarantee you'll get the same results, nobody can guarantee that.
But the extra business is costing me almost nothing to generate. Life is good.

I showed these results to other business owners and clients.
Of course, they wanted to know how *they* could get similar results. With their help, we eventually tested these ideas in 42 separate business categories. Every business we tested these strategies in, got great results. Different size towns, different parts of the country, it didn't matter. Everywhere we tried these ideas, they worked.

So I started holding workshops that allowed us to go through every step and answer every question asked. The workshops show everything the audience needs to know to get great results with local online advertising. But very quickly we found out that many of the business owners attending *really* just wanted to know how much we would charge just to do everything *for* them.

I envy you. For the price of a cheap lunch, you are getting everything it took me two years and lots of money to learn. Study this book. Hit the ground running!

You will notice that I don't talk about Twitter, Facebook, or LinkedIn as local online marketing avenues (although there is a reason to have a Facebook business page). There is a reason for that. In my seminars, eventually someone mentions Facebook. I always ask two questions; "How many here, when looking for information on something you want to buy go to Facebook to find the information?" No hands go up.

"When you are looking to buy something, or want information on it, how many use Google, Yahoo, or another search engine?" All hands go up.

I rest my case.

In your town, right now...today...there are between 10 and 100 people who want what you sell, and are actually looking for a place to buy it. There are another 100-1,000 people who are interested in knowing more about what you sell, but are not quite ready to buy...yet. So let's say there are between 110 and 1,100 people who are highly qualified prospects for what you sell. This book is about to attract *them* to your business.

These "ready to buy" customers may never be found by using social media. Most of them will never be found by any type of advertising. *They must come to you.* You have to be the first place they look...*everywhere* they look. You need to be *omnipresent.* (Look *that* up!)

I also am not talking about local Pay Per Click advertising online. If you follow what is in this book, it simply isn't necessary. It isn't even a plus. Your valuable content is what will bring people into your store, ready to buy. I've tested Pay-Per-Click ads locally and nationally (for an internet store I own). Nationally, they made a difference. Locally, they produced such small results that it wasn't worth doing at all.

The only way local Pay Per Click would be of value to you is if your local competition is so vast, and they are *also* internet savvy, that the top organic search results are all locked in. I have never seen this happen.

What results can you expect from using the ideas in this book?

When I'm speaking to groups of business owners, I show many examples of results achieved from using the ideas presented here. You can see these "before" and "after" profiles by going to the Local Profit Geyser website.

But I want to give you a realistic expectation. This type of marketing will *not* flood your local business with thousands of new prospects a month. Frankly, many people reading this book could not handle another *instant* thousand visitors to their local business a month.

This marketing does not give you tons of new *visitors* that you have to now qualify and sell. The marketing described in this book gives you *buyers*, people ready to *give you money*.

These "pre-sold" buyers are each worth hundreds of times more than "visitors". They already want to buy your highest quality products and your most extensive services. They refer the most profitable customers to you. They give you the most profitable repeat business.

The 80-20 Rule.

Every business has this ratio. 80% of your customers generate 20% of your business. Your *best core* 20% of your customers generate 80% of the profit. This system concentrates completely on getting you more of the core, highly profitable 20%, that will give you 80% of the profit.

That is what the majority of my clients (where we do all the work) experience.

Remember, with this marketing, customers will only be coming in to buy what you promote. So I recommend promoting your best quality, high end stuff.

Customers looking for just a price (the least profitable 80%) are not looking for information...they are just looking for a price. The top 20% of buyers (the group that makes you 80% of your profit) is looking for *information*. And the more quality information they get from *you*...the more likely it is that they will buy from *you*. And the more likely they are interested in the best quality, rather than the lowest price.

You need to use the best bait to catch the biggest fish.

And that's exactly what we are going to show you how to do.

Local Online Marketing And What You Need To Know

I do an increasing schedule of seminars to groups of business owners. The first thing I'll ask the audience is this:

"Who here does any paid advertising?".Then I'll ask "Where do you advertise?" Usually the first or second media to be called out is "Yellow Pages"

And I'll ask "Who here have found that less people are going to the Yellow Pages to find you than ten years ago?". Every hand goes up. It's the same across the country.

So, *where* are the customers *going* to find suppliers then?

The internet. Customers are going online in massive numbers. The debate was over years ago. If you own a business and want to keep it, you must use online marketing not just to compete, but to *survive*.

Let's start off with a few important facts about local internet marketing.....

Internet Facts

41% of consumer use locations in their online search.
Example: "Dentist in Dallas Texas"
Almost all online searches are by product, brand name, name of city, name of state, or by a specific question. Nobody searches by the business name, unless they already know the name of your business and just want the phone number. "I'm ranked number one in Google for my business name" is a fool's claim. *Everyone* is ranked #1 for their company name.

73% of all online activity is related to local search (Google)
The closer your business is to the person doing the online search, the more likely your listing will show up in the search. And the closer your business is to the town the local search term is, "bowling balls mansfieldohio", the better.

67% of Americans use local online search to find local businesses (Comscore)
This number is growing every year. Only a third of all Yellow Page searches are in the print Yellow Pages. Over two thirds of all Yellow Page searches are online.

82% of all local searchers follow up with a walk in or a phone call (Comscore)

Customers are going to buy *somewhere*....why not from you?

43% of all searches are local with the intent of buying off line. (Comscore)

Most people would rather buy locally, but ...if they don't *find* you...they cannot *buy* from you. Another truth to this statistic is that there are lots of local people shopping online with the idea of buying *online*. They are shocked when you show up at the top of a local internet search. They simply don't expect a local business to show up in the search engines. And because you are local, and they can talk to a real person, they will stop by or call you, ready to buy.

We get several high end sales a week because of this one fact alone.

There are two things people look for online besides entertainment; to *learn* about something or to *buy* something.

The vast majority go online to *learn more* before they decide to buy.
The *learning* stage may take several months. The *buying* stage takes a few days, or less. You multiply your effective advertising results if you attract people in both the learning and buying stages. The flaw in any offline advertising is that you ignore the majority of people in the *learning* stage.

I grew my business on these offline "buy now" advertising strategies. They serve me well. *But I was missing the vast majority of online shoppers who were still in some stage of the information gathering process.*

In fact, here is the normal way local people buy.
1) Decide that they want something, or need something.

2) Go online for information about solution alternatives (Getting information).

3) Stay online to shop prices and models (Getting information).

4) Stay online to check out reviews and ask friends online for opinions (Getting information).

5) They decide to buy, locally if possible. Online if convenient (Buying).

Of course, some people have already decided to buy *before* they go online, usually these are impulse items, or popular items that they just *must* buy. For these people there are a large number of online search directories, like several Yellow Page directories and local maps.

But the vast majority of online browsers want to use the internet to *learn* something *before* they decide to buy. The problem is that you are not the one providing them with the answers they seek. If they can't find the information online from *you*, they will find it from (Gasp!)...Your slimy competitor.

If someone does a Google search, and finds, on page one, 5 business listings and 5 free articles answering their specific questions where will they go first?

People's eyes are drawn to video first, articles second and business listings third. They are searching for free information on their subject of interest. They will click on the source of the free information. Why? Because information on the internet is *FREE*.

Articles and videos offer something of value, information. Business listings offer a little more than the name of the business.

Here is the key statement you need to remember; You want the customers at the "information gathering stage" to learn *from you*...to get the information *from you*...to think of *you* as the "Go To" guy....to see *you as the expert*...not pitching a product, but *giving them expert advice*.

But how will they find you?

When they are searching the internet for information on their subject, you want to be omnipresent. Every place they look for information...you want that information search to lead to YOU. You want hundreds of information sources recommending YOU...leading back to YOU...pointing to YOU.

YOU-EVERYWHERE-NOW

There are three main ways customers will find out about you online:
1) By searching online Yellow Pages, or other directories.
2) By using search engines for a local search, to get free information
3) By searching video sites to watch videos on your subject matter.

Remember This; Online Yellow Pages (or similar directories), Local search engine searches, or Video site searches...These are how customers look for you.

No matter which media they choose, you need to be *there*.

The four parts to the entire Marketing System consist of:

Your website: This houses your videos, articles, contact information, Frequently Asked Question Page, and more. This gives you a place for your local search listing to send the prospect *to*. This is where the selling is done. Of course, you sell when they call you or visit your store, but the website *prepares them to buy* from you.

Online Yellow Page and similar directories: For people ready to buy and just looking for a supplier. Most books on local online marketing stop with this one single method. These directory listings account for 3% of my new customer sales created from online sources.

Articles, Blogs, and Reviews: Articles, whether they take the form of blogs, reviews, or press releases, are the engine that drives all your content online. Search engines can read the articles. Articles provide great links to your website. People who show up after they have read your article (or articles) are ready to buy. Writing articles is almost effortless, they are easy to post online, and they are *free* sources for customers. 46% of my local customers generated online say that they came in after reading an article I wrote and posted one of my websites, blog, or PR site.

Video: Videos are short greetings to customers and snippets of information that creates excitement about what you sell. YouTube is so popular now that it is the second largest search engine. If you sell a product that you can show live, video is for you. Want to show graphs? Explain in person? Demonstrate a feature? Videos are for you. You'll see how creating and uploading a video is almost effortless, is free, and creates excitement about your business and what you sell. 51% of my local sales generated online are from people telling me they watched a video of mine online. Some of these people drive up to 100 miles after watching a video. Amazing. And the first time a customer tells you they drove 100 miles *just to talk to you*, you'll be amazed too. The people who come in my store, after they have seen one of my demonstration videos, are pre-sold. After answering a few questions, I just write them up. *Nobody* drives 100 miles unless they have already decided to buy from you.

Why Search Engine Optimization (SEO) Is *Not* The Solution To *Local* Online Marketing

We all continue reading about the subject of Search Engine Optimization. At a local level, is this a good marketing choice to spend your money with? Presented here is why I think there is a better way.

SEO experts can usually get your website listing near the top of the search engines. This process is necessary when you are selling from your website, and selling nationally or internationally. When you are competing with thousands of other dealers on a national scale, you need to be listed near the top, and certainly on page one of a national Google search. And one of the ways to get to the top of a national Google search result…when competing with thousands of other websites, is to create links from other websites to your own website.

So, when you are selling from your website, on a national scale, SEO is *the* way to go.

But for *local* online search engine dominance, SEO isn't the best way.

An SEO expert is only trying to get your *one* listing... (your website listing) ranked highly in the search engines.

And here is a problem; practically no one is looking for your website! People are looking for answers to their questions, information on product comparisons, product reviews, and solutions to a problem. Your website listing, *no matter what its position is*, simply does not give customers what they want.

And your website listing is just one listing. It will be competing with nine other listings on the first page of a local Google search, no matter what position your listing is.

Local shoppers are going online for two reasons (after entertainment). They want to learn something before they buy, or buy something now. And over 95% of these people are still in the "gathering information" stage of the buying progression.

The sizable majority go online to *learn more* before they decide to buy.

The learning stage may take several months. The buying stage takes a few days, or less. You multiply your effective advertising results if you attract people in both the learning and buying stages. The flaw in any offline advertising is that you ignore the majority of people who are still in the learning period. (I know I just repeated myself from the introduction. But you need to hear this now)

If you were thinking of buying something sold locally, and you were looking online, what would you click on...a business listing...or an article that promises to answer the *exact question* you were thinking when you went online?

People will nearly universally click on the link that promises them useful information. Why? Because 95% of the people going online are still in the "information gathering" stage before they make a purchase...and free information is ...well.... it's FREE.

As I said before, in your town, there are people who want to buy what you sell...today. You want to attract *these* people. You want these people to see you are the expert, the "Go To" Guy, who can solve their problems.

And you want these people to see your information *everywhere* they look online.

And you don't want them going anywhere else!

If you can list articles, reviews, videos on Google's local page one search results....you will *own* your local online advertising media.

That would be a *Game Changer*.

Let's get started.

Your Local Website

You can promote your local business online without a business website, but you are at a disadvantage. Every directory listing can include your website URL. Every article, review, post, and e-mail can include your website URL. Your local website acts as a giant brochure that describes what you sell, and why people should buy from you.

A decent website can be built for the cost of domain name registration (about $10 a year), and hosting (about $50 a year). Buyers can visit your website to find customer testimonials, photos, videos, articles about what you do, audio, and your contact information. Not having a website for your local business is like not having a phone.

Customers expect you to have a website, and not having one signals them that you are not serious about wanting their business. Besides, your nearest competitor has one.

Your URL

Your URL is the actual website name or domain name. For example www.website.com

Here is a mistake almost every merchant makes. They name the URL of their website the same as the business name. That's a perfectly natural thing to do, but you can get far more value out of your URL if you use search words (keywords) in your domain name.

Here is something you should know about your URL; it is the first thing search engines look at when they are placing you in search listing results. Your potential customers are looking online for what you sell or the service you provide. They are not looking for the name of your business.

For example, in my retail business the search words are usually "vacuum cleaners" or "Vacuum cleaners Wooster Ohio". Nobody ever thinks to type in "The Sweeper Store"(The name of my store) in a local search when looking to buy a vacuum cleaner. If they already knew the name of your store, they wouldn't be looking in a search engine; they would use the Yellow Pages. So I have two websites for local searches. One I built using the name of my business as the URL (this is way before I knew what I was doing), and a website that has its URL as:"vacuumcleanerswoosterohio.com".

So now, when people search for "vacuum cleaners Wooster Ohio" the first thing that pops up in the local search results is my website. You can do the same. Get a domain name that contains the most popular search words for what you sell. That's smart, and you will be the only one in your area dong it. We use www.GoDaddy.com for our domain name registering.

Hosting

Hosting is simply where you park your website. GoDaddy has website hosting. We use www.HostGator.comYou can host dozens of websites for just $12.95 a month. Sweet.

Title tags, description tags

Your website Title Tag tells the search engines what your website is about. Your title tag shows up above the website in a little window. The default Title Tag is usually the website URL, which is a mistake. Your Title Tag is also what shows up as the headline when your website is listed on a Google search. My Title tag is "VacuumCleanersWoosterOhio | We Sell Vacuums, Parts, And More!". That way, anyone who uses search phrases that contain any of the words in my title tag, will see my listing at or near the top. When we build a website for a client, we always use popular search words in the website URL, in the title tag, and in the description.

Description tags are what the viewer sees after your title tag and domain name. Here is an example of all three;

VacuumCleanersWoosterOhio | We Sell Vacuums, Parts, And More!
vacuumcleanerswoosterohio.com/
Shopping for **vacuum cleaners**, ceiling fans, heaters, or air purifiers? **Wooster Ohio** shoppers buy their **vacuum cleaner** parts, HEPA filters, **vacuum cleaner** bags, ...

Your description tag needs to be a real sentence or two. Don't just use sentence fragments. And do not fall into the trap of just using search words repeatedly. Google will see that as Spam, and delete your listing. The description can use as many search words as you can fit in as long as the description sounds natural.

Search terms and key words

Search terms, search words, search phrases, and key words all mean the same thing. This is what an internet shopper types in a search engine like Google to find information they want.

A smart idea is to go to Google's keyword tool. Just search Google for "Google Keyword Tool" The first result is what you want. You will be able to see how many searches are done for each search word, or search term. Pick the most relevant to what you sell, and with the most monthly searches, and make sure you include these words in your descriptions and website content.

Something you should do is go online and search for a product you sell or a service you provide. Look at the top website listings. These titles and descriptions got that business to the top of the search engine. Study the first few listings. They can teach you a lot. Copy the best parts of each.

Content on your home page

On your actual website home page, there are a few things that will make the search engines love your site and rank it higher in the search engines. Take your search terms that are most popular and put them on your website as often as you can, while making the text read naturally. If you take the five or ten most popular search terms for your business, you can weave them all in the text without making the text look like you are "Keyword stuffing".

A few hints:

Put your best keywords early on the home page. The first sentence is a good place for them.

Earlier in sentences is better than at the end of sentences. "Vacuum Cleaners; Which feature is best for you?" is far better than "Which feature is best when looking for a Vacuum Cleaner". This also applies to headlines on any articles written for your website.Photos and video do not count to search engines. Print counts.

The first paragraph on your site should tell what you do, why someone should buy from you, and make the reader want to read further.

Try to get at least 500 words on your homepage. And make sure your main keyword makes up less than 1% of the words on your homepage.

On your home page, of your local business website, you should have the following:

A welcome video

Or at least a welcome *audio* with your voice. The video should be of you welcoming the viewer to your website and business. This short (5 minutes or less) video will start the process of creating a relationship with the visitor. Make the video conversational, not a serious recital.

Videos of product demonstrations, testimonials, reviews

You should be in the video (or at least your voice). These videos create value in what you sell, and establish you as the "Go To" guy. These videos will also be posted to video sites like YouTube.com.

These videos should draw the customer into your store or at least to the phone to call you. Real information should be in these videos, not just promotional hype. A few videos are enough, and a few minutes each is enough. Make sure your contact information is on the video itself. These videos will be spread out across the internet without the text on your home page. So your contact information needs to be in the video. Under the videos, on your home page, you will need to add a description of what is in the video.

At the bottom of your home page you will put your contact information, store hours, days open, map, and directions to your business.

A Frequently Asked Questions page

At the top of your home page, you will need a menu. One link should be to your Frequently Asked Questions page. Here is where you ask virtually every question a customer could ask or should ask, along with your answer. A lot of confidence in buying from you is built here. Here is where you put all your terms of doing business. At the bottom of this page, put a link back to the home page.

An Articles link at the bottom of the home page

We will talk about the value of articles, and how to write them painlessly in a minute.

How To Get Your Website Ranked Highly

We are going to spend very little time on Search Engine Optimization here. In national online selling, it matters more because you are competing with maybe thousands of bright, savvy, marketers. But we are concentrating on local online marketing.

With local marketing, it's far more important to get your *content* (articles, video, etc.) listed on search engines for local searches. But these tips will help your *website* show up earlier in a local online search.

---

1) Title tags. Make sure your title tag says what you do, and includes the most popular search words that apply to what you sell.

2) Description tags. Make sure your description is a real sentence that is about 200 characters long. Make sure it describes the benefit of going to your website. The Title tag and description tag won't actually show up on your website. They are typed in when your website is being built. The title and description tags are what the search engines list in local searches pointing to your website.

3) Your Domain name (or URL). Use keywords in your domain name. This may be the single surest way to guarantee your website will come up early in local searches.

4) First paragraph should contain plenty of different search phrases.

5) Make sure there is plenty of keyword rich content on your home page. Also, use links in your "Menu" on the home page to link to additional written content on your website, like a Frequently Asked Questions page, and additional articles.

Getting one way links to your website.

The surest way to get better rankings on your website is to get plenty of *one way relevant links from* websites online. Read that again. "One way links" means that another website links to you, but you don't link back to them. Google values one way links far more than reciprocal links. (Reciprocal links means that you exchange links with the other website).

Here are guaranteed ways to get plenty of one way links:

Use website directories.

You can get lists of website directories by just typing in "Website directories" on Google. You will get plenty of free options. There is software that will make registering with these directories a little faster, but it will be manual labor regardless.

You want links from other websites (not directories) to be relevant to what you do. If you sell teddy bears, you want links from other websites that talk about teddy bears too.

This will also help in your marketing. People who are visiting a teddy bear website, will also be interested in your teddy bear site. You can contact the site to exchange links, or provide that site with an article about teddy bears with your website URL at the end of the article.

A proven way to get one way links to your website is to post videos on video sites (like YouTube.com). Make sure you put your website URL in the video description. And be sure to include your URL in your profile.

Videos on these sites also help your marketing, because people interested in your subject matter will follow the article and video links back to your website to learn more about what you do. This will happen across the country, but your articles and videos will show up much earlier in a local search.

Commenting on Blogs and Forums

If you find a Forum that discusses what you sell or a Blog on your subject, you can leave comments. In your comment you have a "signature" that has your name, business name, and URL. This will usually provide an additional link to your website, but it will also lead people back to your website to see and hear your sales story.

Don't overdo this. Leaving 100 comments on a forum only counts as one link to Google.

The same with Blogs. You want to leave informative, useful, relevant comments on many forums and Blogs...more comments on one Blog may bring more people to your website, but won't count as multiple links.

Again, let me remind you that in local online marketing, the most important strategy is to plaster your content (written and video) all over the internet for search engines to find. It is this content that will bring you the most buyers. But getting your website placed highly in a local search (very easy with the right domain name) is useful too... so I gave you things I have done to help with this.

"Positioning: When an angry dog runs at you, clap your hands, smile, and say 'Here Boy!'"

-Claude Whitacre

Your Local Search Directory Listings

This is your online Yellow Page listings, Google Business, Yelp, Bing, and City Search.
You are probably listed with most of these online directories already. What we want to do here is show you how to claim your listing. You will see how to add information to make your listing more attractive to search engines (and customers), and how to add your listing everywhere it could possibly be listed, all for free.

The two kinds of searches that show up in a Google search are the Google Business results at the very top. These are just local business listings with a common map with locators on it. Then the next eight or ten listings are the search engine results, that contain directory listings, video, articles, reviews, and snippets of content from every online source.

On the next page you will see a screenshot of the Google listings for the search phrase "auto repair wooster".

The first seven listings are the Google Business Local listings. The three listings at the bottom are the natural organic listings for the search phrase.

Your placement in the Google Business Local listings is based on your location, number of reviews posted, and number of identical listings in other search directories.

Al-Rite **Automotive**
www.alrite**automotive**.com/
2 Google reviews

(A) 1050 Grosjean Road
Wooster
(330) 262-8268

Kauffman Tire
www.kauffmantire.com/
2 Google reviews

(B) 519 Madison Avenue
Wooster
(330) 264-1781

Spurgeon Chevrolet
www.spurgeonchevrolet.com/
1 Google review

(C) 1119 West Old Lincoln
Way
Wooster
(330) 264-2300

Smetzer's Tire Center, Inc.
www.smetzertire.com/
Google+ page

(D) 352 West Liberty Street
Wooster, Ohio
(330) 264-9901

Monro Muffler Brake & **Service**
find.monro.com/**auto-repair**/.../177/?...
3 Google reviews

(E) 2781 Cleveland Road
Wooster
(330) 345-6310

Aber **Automotive** Inc
plus.google.com
Google+ page

(F) 1023 Blachleyville Road
Wooster
(330) 264-0573

300 Tire Services
www.300tire.com/
1 Google review

(G) 210 South Buckeye
Street
Wooster
(330) 262-6800

More results near **Wooster, OH** »

Oil Change - Towing - Muffler - Transmission Repair - Tire Dealers

Automobile - Repairs & Services in **Wooster**, OH - AOL Yellow Pages
yellowpages.aol.com/**auto-repair**/oh/**wooster**/
10+ items – Find great **Automobile - Repairs** & Services in **Wooster**, OH ...
Meineke **Car** Care Centers 866-205-7340 | Official Website www.meineke ...
Park Mazda of **Wooster** 330-345-8506 | Official Website | Directions | Send ...

Wooster auto repair - Columbus Local Business Directory
oh-directory.hometownlocator.com › Ohio Gazetteer
Results 1 - 15 of 696 – **auto repair** for **Wooster**, OH. Find phone numbers, addresses,
maps, driving directions and reviews for **auto repair** in **Wooster**, OH.

Top Maintenance and **autoRepair** in **Wooster**, OH. Call Monro today!
find.monro.com/**Auto-Repair**/OH/Cleveland/177
Monro is your #1 source reliable for **auto repair** and maintenance in **Wooster**, OH,
providing tune ups, alignments, oil changes, brakes repair and more. Stop in ...

Your listings are very important to you. Online search listings usually come from only a couple of sources; Search engines or online directories.

Have you ever used the Yellow Pages to find a pizza? How many Yellow Page directories did you look in to find a pizza? The answer is always "One".

Consumers will search *One* online Yellow Page directory or search *One* Search Engine.

If you are listed in *that* directory *first*, you get the call. Go to YP.com which is the online Yellow Page listings.

If your prospect uses a search engine, you better be in the first few positions, or *you lose*. You need to be everywhere a prospect could possibly search.

If they use a local directory, you must be listed first or second.
If they do a Google search, you must be listed on page one...*preferably several times*.

You want your sales information and business listings showing up so often that you virtually crowd out your competition.

Claiming Your Google Listings

Amazingly, if you have not claimed your listing, a competitor can claim your listing, and add whatever information they like. Your listed phone number could be changed so that all incoming calls could go to his business. Your website URL could be replaced with his.

Do this now; Go to www.moz.com/local. You can check the major directories to make sure your listing is correct, and/or claim your listing. It will only take a minute. Just type in the name of your business and your zip code.

What your listing can include.
You can just list your business, without a website, or with a website. The more places you are listed, the more likely you will show up on page one (maybe multiple times) on a Google search.

Most listings also have spaces to list the following;
- Products and services you offer.
- Brands you carry.
- Directions to your business.
- A video (that you create) to promote your business.
- Up to five pictures of your choice to create familiarity with your business.
- Your store hours.
- What credit cards you accept, and credit terms you offer.
- Complete descriptions of each product line you carry.
- A direct link so customers can e-mail you.
- Any logos, certifications, or awards you have won are listed.

Moz.com/local's major directory claiming page

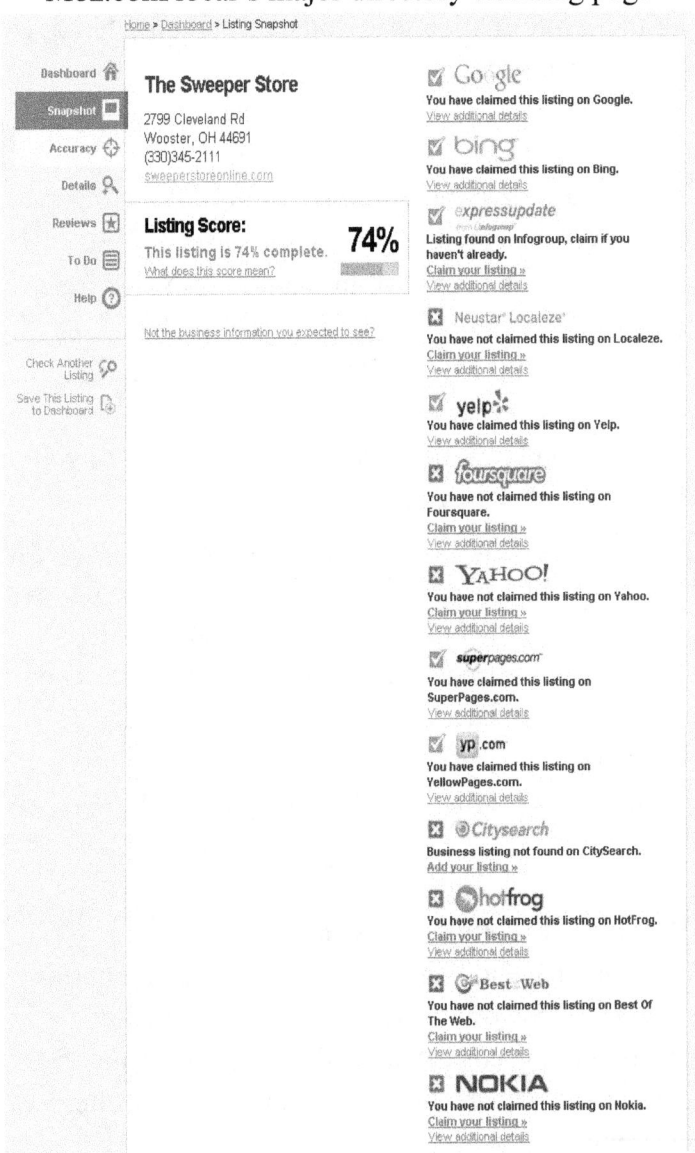

Many of these directories will allow you to include far more information than you could fit on a full page Yellow Page ad.

The advantages these online "company profiles" have over a print Yellow Page ad are:

- You can change anything in the listing for free, whenever you need to.
- Your "company profile" isn't being seen right next to all your main local competitors.
- You can have the customer click directly to your video sales message.
- They can click directly to an audio sales message.
- You are not listed alphabetically online, but based on the number of places you are listed with identical listings, and the number of reviews you have received.
- A map to your business is included in every business profile. You'll be easy to find!

Where to submit your listings

You may have a listing in several online directories already. What you want to do is make sure the information is correct, and add any information the directory will accept to make yourself look better to a customer.

Each directory will have a simple icon on its home page to show you where to check your listing. Some of these listings you can check on www.getlisted.org.

There are others though.

www.google.com/business
The granddaddy of them all. You must be here. This one listing will count for half of the local online searches.

www.local.yahoo.com
Just scroll to the bottom of the home page and click "Add/Edit Business"

www.bing.com/businessportal
Look to the right of the homepage. You can "sign in" or click the "Get Started Now!" button.

www.yelp.com
On the homepage; click "Create Your Free Account" to get started.

www.yp.com
This is the main online Yellow Pages Directory.

Remember, the purpose of going to these sites is not just to see if you have a listing, sometimes you will. The purpose here is to *claim your listing*, and add whatever additional information you can. Online browsers will trust you more, the more information they see. Also, search engines give your website more credence when your business information is in lots of different directories. It makes your business seem more established the more places it is listed.

And remember, every listing with your website URL is another link to your website.

One of the main reasons to submit your business profile to everyplace you can is that Google will post your listings from the directories that have the most complete information. This is why, when you do a local Google search, you will see search results with directory listings from so many different directories. The more places you submit your business profile, the better chance for a complete business profile to show up early in the search.

But no matter how many places you post your business listing, it will only show up *once* in a search engine search.

On the next page is a Google page one search for "vacuum cleaners dallas texas". Look at all the different directories listed. These are very boring listings to a viewer.

LocalProfitGeyser.com

ɔogle | vacuum cleaners dallas texas

Web   Images   Maps   Shopping   More ▾   Search tools

About 817,000 results (0.39 seconds)

Dallas Vacuum cleaners repair service - Yellowpages.com
www.yellowpages.com/**dallas-tx**/**vacuum-cleaners**-repair-service
Results 1 - 30 of 46 – 46 listings of **Vacuum Cleaners**-Repair & Service in **Dallas** on
YP.com. Find reviews, directions & phone numbers for the best vacuum ...

Best **Dallas Vacuum Cleaners** | Angie's List
www.angieslist.com › Local Reviews › TX › Dallas
DALLAS, **TX**. Find Dallas **Vacuum Cleaners** on Angie's List. 128. Dallas **Vacuum
Cleaners** are on Angie's List. Top Rated Dallas **Vacuum Cleaners** on Angie's ...

AAA Vacuum Cleaner CO (Aaa **Vacuum Cleaner**) - **Dallas, Texas** ...
www.manta.com/c/mm2rzgj/aaa-**vacuum-cleaner**-co
AAA **Vacuum Cleaner** CO company profile in **Dallas**, **TX**. Our free company profile
report for AAA **Vacuum Cleaner** CO includes business information such as ...

Find BBB Accredited Industrial **Vacuum Cleaner** Suppliers in **Dallas** ...
www.bbb.org/**dallas**/.../vacuum-cleaners-industrial-and-comm...
Find BBB Accredited Industrial **Vacuum Cleaner** Suppliers in **Dallas Texas** - your
guide to trusted **Dallas Texas** Industrial **Vacuum Cleaner** Suppliers, ...

Vacuum Cleaners in **Dallas, TX** - Business Yellow Pages by WFAA
directory.wfaa.com/**vacuum-cleaners/dallas/tx**
Read and write reviews on Dallas **Vacuum Cleaners**. Get phone numbers, ratings,
maps, directions and more for **Vacuum Cleaners** in **Dallas**, **TX**. Powered by ...

Vacuum Cleaner Repair in **Dallas, TX** - Business Yellow Pages by ...
directory.wfaa.com/**vacuum-cleaner**-repair/**dallas/tx**
Read and write reviews on Dallas **Vacuum Cleaner** Repair. Get phone numbers,
ratings, maps, directions and more for **Vacuum Cleaner** Repair in **Dallas**, **TX**.

AAA **Vacuum Cleaner** Co - 9845 Walnut Hill Ln **Dallas, TX, 75238**
directory.wfaa.com/biz/.._vacuum-cleaner.../dallas/tx/.../12031...
Reviews and ratings of AAA **Vacuum Cleaner** Co at 9845 Walnut Hill Ln **Dallas**, **TX**,
75238. Get phone numbers, maps, directions and addresses for AAA ...

Dallas, TX Vacuum Cleaners on Citysearch
dallas.citysearch.com/.../**dallas-tx**/vacuum_cleaners/71473_12...
Dallas, TX - Masters Supply Source in Dallas
Citysearch® helps you find **Vacuum Cleaners** in **Dallas**, **TX**.
4. Vacumaid of North **Texas**   9884 Monroe Dr   32.877739   96.878039
7. Aaa **Vacuum Cleaner** Co   9845 Walnut Hill Ln   32.879373   96.716178

Goooooooooogle ›

1 2 3 4 5 6 7 8 9 10   **Next**

Advanced search   Search Help   Give us feedback

Google Home   Advertising Programs   Business Solutions   Privacy & Terms
About Google

54

Tips that will help you get high placement in Google…

These factors will count in where any search engine will rank your business listing.

Claiming your Google Plus Local listing:
This is very important. Do this right away, for security reasons and to help your rankings.

Customer Reviews:
Any customer review on your directory listings will help search engines decide how substantial your business is for their listings. If you get a bad review, get three of your best customers to write a great review. They will be glad to help, and it will make them a teensy bit famous.

Your business address in the city the search is being conducted:
If your business is listed as being in the same city as the search is being conducted, you get better search results.

Consistent information:
Your listing should have the same spelling, the same names, and the same address in every listing. It counts against you if the information is different from listing to listing.

An 800 toll free number in your listing helps.

A website listed helps. (Always list the same website)

Having a real address helps a lot. Do not use PO Boxes for listings. Use a real address. Use your home address if you have to. If you have an address with a box number, use "Suite" instead of "box".

Use keywords in your business listing descriptions, but do not overdo it. Spamming is frowned upon, and will get your listing deleted.

Here are a few things that will hurt your rankings:
- Not showing an address in your listings.
- Using a PO Box as an address
- Trying to create multiple listings with any of the same information.
- Trying to list your business multiple times with the same title.
- Again, spamming keywords is bad.

There is one downside to claiming and updating your free listings. All of these online directories sell advertising. The list they call is the list you just got on by being active on your listing. You will get a phone call...

And when you do get a call, and you hear, (after a few seconds of dead time) "Hello, This is Bob calling about your internet Yellow Pages"... hang up. This is a call selling a listing you already have and adding one website page for charges between $49-$69 a month. I get 5-15 of these calls a *day*. I always hang up. These charges will show up on your phone bill without your authorization, and you'll have to fight to get them off. No matter what you tell them on the phone, they will call back relentlessly. If you came in my store, and saw me answer the phone and immediately hang up without saying a word...it was one of these calls.

If you get a call saying; "Hello, this is Mary calling from Superpages.com. You recently submitted a listing".This is a legitimate call from one of the directories. I'm polite, and always say "I just want the standard listing". They are just doing their job to tell you about an enhanced listing. It only takes a minute, and they won't call you back.

I would absolutely suggest you never buy an enhanced listing. Your local listing will show up depending on the information you provide and the number of directories you are listed in. None of these directories will *individually* give you high rankings. At rates of $49 a month and up to $1100 *each*, you would be spending $10,000 a month or more in total for "enhanced listings" for maybe one more call a month from a prospect.

Remember, these are *local* listings. You are going to show up early in the listings anyway, as long as you submit the right information. Please, please don't spend your money here.

Reps calling you from business directories will tell you "We can get your business listed #1". This is true, but they can only get you listed #1 *in their directory*.

Your position in Google, Yahoo, or Bing will not change if you buy a featured listing, Even if you pay $1,000 a month for the privilege.

"Either write something worth reading or do something worth writing about"

-Benjamin Franklin

Your Local Written Content

Why write articles?

You should have at least several articles written and placed on your website before you submit them to article sites. Personally, I put a list of article titles at the bottom of the home page. Each title is a link to the actual article on another page on my website.

"But Claude, I can't write articles!".
I hear that in every workshop I give.

Have you ever had a customer ask you a question about what you sell?

Did you give an answer that took two or three minutes?

The question they asked was the *title* to the article.

The answer you gave was the *article itself.*

See how easy that was?

The easy, fast, and painless way to write an article?

In your Frequently Asked Questions page on your website, you should have two kinds of questions; questions about your business, and your business policies...and questions that help a customer decide which decision is best for them.

Examples of these questions are:

"What should I look for when buying a _____?"

"What features give which advantages?"

"How can I tell if I even need a _____?"

"What would be the solution to this (specify) problem?"

These questions and their answers make great articles. Every time a customer asks you a question that you think would interest others, write it down. The answer you give practically writes itself.

You can see articles that I wrote for my customers at my store website at:
www.vacuumcleanerswoosterohio.com

Where to get your article posted so the search engines will find it?
Always post articles on your website first. Then post the article on your blog (Unless your blog *is* your website). Make your articles at least 500 words and only post one article on a website page. At the bottom of the article, link it back to the home page of your website.

There are about 1,000 article distribution websites out there. They don't charge to post your article. They make their money by selling ad space on their website. Other websites find your articles and post them across the internet. The better the article, the more people spread it around.

Just go on Google and type in "Article submission site lists", and you'll get more than enough to keep you busy. The only drawback to submitting to multiple sites is that you have to register, by hand, for every article site. A few hours well spent.

A couple of the top article distribution sites I highly recommend are:

- EzineArticles.com
- ArticleDashboard.com
- HubPages.com
- Articles.org

These article sites all have different acceptance criteria. Most want articles between 500-800 words. This is about one full page typed on a Word program.

The main rule is to not promote your business in the article itself, but provide useful information and save the promoting for the "author's box" after the article itself.

Here is what an article looks like after it is posted:

Vacuum Cleaners - Service Or Replace?

By *Claude Whitacre*

 How long your vacuum will last has to do with the quality of the vacuum in the first place. If you buy an inexpensive vacuum cleaner from a discount chain or big box store, you have to understand that these vacuums are not made to be serviced. They are made to be used and disposed of when they have problems. These vacuums are made to last two or three years. With careful use they can last much longer.

Vacuums sold by independent vacuum retailers are generally better quality because the dealer also services the vacuums. So the dealers will tend to want to sell vacuums that will not be thrown out, but will get regular service.

Generally, when a complete repair is equal to half the cost of replacement, it's time to replace the vacuum.

Here is how to make your vacuum last longer;

Make sure the belt is tight around the roller brush. If you use your fingers to "spin" the roller while it has the belt on, and the belt slips, it's time to replace the belt. Never do this while the vacuum cleaner is on.

Check your bag and filters. If your bag is more than half full, change it. A completely full vacuum cleaner bag will restrict the air flow that cools the motor. Your motor will overheat and need to be replaced. In most cases, and motor replacement is over half the cost of a new vacuum cleaner. If you filter is dirty over its entire surface, change it. This will also restrict airflow.

If you have pets that shed, or someone in your home has long hair, check the roller brush every several months to make sure hair did not get stuck in the roller bearings. If the hair has wound around a bearing, use a knife to get the hair out. Obviously, do this with the vacuum unplugged.

Vacuums are usually made of some grade of plastic. All plastic will break if slammed hard enough into the walls. Use your vacuum with care. Show anyone else who will be using the vacuum how to use it. In our store in Wooster Ohio, 90% of our repairs come in from people loaning their vacuum out to a friend or relative. Make sure they know how to take care of it.

Your vacuum will last for ten years or more. if serviced regularly. Take it into a vacuum retailer for annual service. The belt, bag (or filter) should be replaced at least once a year.

Ask you dealer what services are free.

Vacuum cleaner expert reviewer Claude Whitacre owns The Sweeper Store in Wooster Ohio.

You can see vacuum reviews at [http://www.vacuumcleanerswoosterohio44691.com] or see the store website at http://www.sweeperstoreonline.com

What to write about.

Earlier, I showed you how to use your FAQ page for article ideas.

You want the article to be about something the customer would ask themselves before they decided to buy. It could be about features to look for, a comparison with a competitive product, options available to solve their problem, the history (or a small section of it) of your industry, lists of tips in buying what you sell, etc.

The chief rule is to make it interesting to the reader who is thinking about what you sell.

The single most important part of your article is your headline.

The headline is what determines where the article is placed in an online search.

The headline determines if a prospective customer reads the article or not.

In almost every case, the only thing the reader has available to decide if they want to read your article...is the headline.

The closer your headline matches what the prospect types in as a search word or phrase...the higher up your article will show in the search results.

Useful article titles are:

"(Product name): The Top Ten Ways To Benefit From Your New (product name slightly differently said)"

"(Product name); What To Look For When Shopping For A New One"

"(Product name): What Features Will Benefit You Most?"

"Is (Product name) Really The Best (Product category)?"

"The (Product name) Product Review"

"(Product name): A Quick History"

What to not include in your article

If you write promotional copy in your article, it will be declined.

Take out "I" as often as you can and replace it with "You". The article isn't about you; it's about how the reader can get what *they* want.

Do not include your links in the article itself. This will get the article declined almost always. If you include a link, make sure it really helps the reader, and the link has nothing to do with you.

Never send duplicate articles (the same article to the same article site). You can send the same article to different article sites, if you wish, but never send the same article to the same place twice. This is considered Spam and will get your account with that site banned.

Your author box; How to promote your business

This is separate from your article. Your author Box will contain your website links (maximum of two) your company name and address, your phone (if you like), and a very short biography. A hundred words are plenty for this.

How to make sure your articles pop up on a local search

Your article title and author box are what show up usually in Google searches.

So you want your title to have the precise words in it that the most popular searches (in your category) have. You want to make sure that you list your city and state in your author box. If you don't, the *search engines will have no way of knowing where "Local" is to you.* This is an absolute must if you want our articles to show up in local searches.

Why search engines love articles

Search engines can *read* articles. They cannot read videos or pictures.

Search engines are dedicated to providing useful content when an internet user does an online search. Useful content is *information*. Useful content is not advertising.

And articles, by their very nature, contain lots of useful content per square inch. So the search engines favor article in searches. Your article may be listed in the number one position out of five thousand search results...if it's the only article. (And if the headline matches the search exactly)

Your articles will contain far more information for Google to read, post, and rank, than any other format like video and business listings.

Extend your market area. Multiply your prospects.

Before I started posting useful articles and videos to promote my retail store, I would have a market area that spread out about five miles from my store. Occasionally, someone would drive twenty miles. After I posted the videos and added the articles, my market area expanded. I didn't do this on purpose; it was just an effect of placing articles and video online.

Here is why your market will expand when you post useful videos and articles. *Because you will be the only person in your industry, in your area, doing this.*

Now we have customers routinely traveling 30 miles to see us. We get several customers a month traveling from the edges of Ohio (our store is located in north central Ohio). This is over 100 miles.

This "expanding market effect" was not planned; it was an effect of posting valuable (in the search engine's eyes) content.

After we saw that people would actually drive from way out of our area, we decided to attract those people on purpose.

Here is what we did:
I included their city and state in the title of the article. This will greatly increase your chances of the article showing up on the first page of Google in that city.

Why would someone drive 100 miles to see you, when there are suppliers next door to them?

The stronger the relationship, the more unique the offer, the more information gathered, and the more time the customer has invested in your content, the further they will travel to see you. Because they think you are the *only one* who can help them.

Your articles and videos show up in searches much further away, than just your listing.
Because you are the only one writing and posting this kind of information.

You can write articles about every single product you sell, not just about your business.
Articles are literally the same as a full page newspaper advertisement. And you could write one about every single thing you sell. And the ad runs *forever*.

How to write reviews that get posted and read by eager buyers.

Call your article a Review. Put the word "Review" in the article title. Review products you sell. After all, you're an expert. Don't review yourself, or your own business. Your article will be rejected.

Now, about the online reviews. The reason there are no online reviews about any specific product is that...in the English speaking world...*not one dealer* has taken the time to write a product review, call it a Review, and post it online.

There is nothing wrong with sellers writing reviews on products they sell. As long as the review is accurate and not just a sales pitch, it will be welcomed on any number of websites that post reviews.

This is not immoral, unethical, or evil. It's simply a way to impart knowledge to the public.

Aren't you an expert on what you sell? So am I. As an expert, our opinion carries weight.

Reviews are articles. If you put the word "Review" in the title, it's a review. If review sites see the article (many are on a feed for such things), they will post it.

Here is how to make this unethical:

Review your own business. You cannot review your own business in the same way you can't recommend yourself for a promotion, or write a review of your own book. I also don't recommend going to product review websites, reviewing a product you sell, and passing yourself off as a consumer. That's sleazy, and you may get caught. Do you want great reviews on your business? Do you want great reviews on review sites? That's what grateful customers and friends are for.

You also need to say, somewhere in the article or signature (that thing at the end of the article that says who wrote it) that you are a dealer for the product, or that you own a store that sells the product. Reviews don't have to be written by customers, they can also be written by experts. That's you.

You can literally dominate a local online search for a specific product by writing a few articles about your product or service, and submitting them to these article sites. They will almost always show up high on a Google search. Google loves articles far more than it does simple business listings. Articles are scanned by Google. The keywords the article contains help place it high in a local Google search.

These review articles can be found nationally. But if you include your city and state in the author's signature box (at the end of the article), the articles will dominate a local online search.

In my area, I have about 12 of these product reviews. These are all products I sell, as I state in the author boxes. These articles along with product demonstration videos and "How to buy a ..." articles cover the entire first page of any local Google search. Why? Is it because I'm so brilliant? No. It's because nobody else in my business, within 1,000 miles will go to the trouble. I even write reviews about vacuum cleaners I don't sell but would take as trade-ins. All these articles draw people into your store, and make you the "Go To Guy" for your business.

Of course, this idea will work in any business, any product, and any industry.

If you are not skilled in spelling or if English is a second language, you may want someone to proofread your articles. Article sites will reject your article if it has too many spelling errors. If you still don't feel like you can write articles, you can hire professional article writers, they normally charge between $50-$150 for a 500 word article. You can find plenty of people willing to write articles for you by going to elance.com.

I recommend you write the articles yourself if possible. That way they are in your own voice, and your personality will show through. The article won't sound so sterile.

One thing about submitting to article submission sites:
The article will eventually be archived. That just means you won't be able to find it in the article site's listings. That's OK, search engines can still find it, especially if the article is also posted on your website. Make sure that *all* your articles are *also posted on your website*, and this will never be a problem.

As long as your website is online, the articles are too.

I learned this next information (unfortunately) *after* I dominated my local search engines.

When building your website, always include your articles on your website first, before you submit them to any article distribution websites. You want Google to crawl your articles on your website, before they see the same article on another site. Why? Because in the listing, you want *your* URL to show up and not the URL (Domain name) of the article website.

Plus, your articles that you placed on your website will never be archived, and the links broken. If the article is on your website, it will be online until the website is shut down.

Your Blog, And Why You Need One.

This is going to be much easier than you think.
Just got to Blogger.com and create a blog. It's free.

Now, why do you need a blog?
Well, the truth it, for local businesses, very few people will actually go to your blog and read your posts. You'll probably get few subscribers.

But here is why a Blog is useful;

Google sees a blog on a different platform (Like Blogger.com) as a different source of information.

Google really only wants to have one or two listings from each platform, for one business. On each page. So, for example, it's difficult to get 5 page one Google search listings with every one of them being an article from your website. It's also difficult to get more than two YouTube videos on a page of Google search results.

So your Blog gives Google another source.

Now, what do you put on your blog? The same articles you put on your website.

Make sure the title to the articles on your Blog includes the type of business you own and the city and state. An example of an article might be titled; "Cleveland Ohio Chiropractor Give Tips On Helping An Aching Back"

Google will see the article title and will know that if someone is in Cleveland Ohio and types in "Chiropractor" or "Aching back" as a search, the article should show up in one of the top positions.

Even the name of your Blog should include the relevant search phrases.

If you are a plumber in Dallas Texas, you may want to title your Blog "Plumbing Tips From Your Dallas Texas Plumber", and your URL could be: www.plumbingblogdallastexas.com

So, what do you include in your Blog post?

If you have a YouTube video on the subject of the post, you can just copy and paste the YouTube link to the video in your blog. It creates a god link to your video, and makes your blog post more attractive to readers.

At the end of every Blog post be sure to include a link to your website, and make sure your contact information is permanently at the heading of the Blog.

"Everything is impossible, until someone does it"
                                        -Unknown

(No idea who said it first...Maybe me.)

Your Facebook Business Page

This is going to be a very short chapter.
Facebook is not a great way for people to find you
online and then buy from you. Local merchants
spend time creating a "Community" of followers on
their Facebook page. And they hope that eventually a
few of those followers will call them and buy
something.

But people don't go on Facebook to buy things. They
go on Facebook for social interaction.

So why have a Facebook Business page? Because Google likes Facebook. Facebook is another platform that Google can list as a source of information. And It's very possible that your Facebook page will show up on the first page of a local Google search, when a local customer is doing research or looking to buy.

So…..what do you put on your Facebook page? The same articles you put in your Blog, which are the same articles you put in your website.

You can change the titles if you like (I do) to allow other search terms to be included in the titles…but it isn't necessary.

You can also post your YouTube videos on Your Facebook page….and on your Blog..and on your website.

On Facebook, you can also post any news that concerns your business…any promotions you are doing, and Birthdays, celebrations, events, or contests.

Your Local Videos And The Purpose Of Your Videos

To provide links to your website and contact information.

A link to your business website from a video hosting site will help in your Google rankings. Of course, the link will also take the viewer to your website. And if you put your contact information in the video, and in its description...it will also get you phone calls direct from someone watching your video. I get several of these calls every day.

To establish yourself as an expert.
Videos give you a platform to share your ideas, give helpful advice, and answer customer's questions. One thing that really surprised me was the credibility my customers gave the fact that I had videos online. To them, I was an expert *because* I was in a video.

To create the beginning of a relationship between you and the customer.
The more the customer hears about you, the more they hear your voice, read your articles, or watch you on a video, the more *famous* you are to them. And all these different ways to obtain your content creates a relationship between you and the customer. This happens even if you personally are not involved. Celebrities get this all the time. A fan thinks they are friends, because of what they have seen on TV for years. They think they *know* the actor. The same thing happens here. Your customers will come to see you with an entirely different attitude than if they never met you. If they read your material or see you online, they feel like there is the beginning of a relationship.

The type of videos that create a rush of buyers coming through your door.

Product selling demonstrations create demand for what you sell. If you can create a short "infomercial" about what you sell, the people coming through your door will be ready to buy. If you need to, you can create several videos of parts for your product demonstration. For example, 5 parts to a 25 minute demonstration. All five parts can be hosted on your website. And each part counts as a separate video to be uploaded to video websites.

What videos *not* to do.

I have to tell you, joke videos don't sell anything. Clever videos, trying to show how clever you are, don't bring anyone to your business. Videos should provide useful suggestions, tips, product comparisons, and solutions to problems. If you have a pet cat who likes to jump through a hoop...this isn't where you show it.

Study infomercials. They are never funny for the sake of being funny. They give "wow" product demonstrations and pack a lot of information in as short of a time as possible.

How to create videos; cheap, fast, and painless.
One way is to simply videotape your Frequently
Asked Questions. Have someone off camera read the
questions, and you answer them on camera. This
should easily get you 15 or20 short videos that you
can post on your website. In fact, your entire FAQ
page could be videos with the questions listed under
each one.

Where to post your videos.
There are several video hosting sites. YouTube.com
is the most well known.

Here are other video websites:
- Veoh.com
- Metacafe.com
- Dailymotion.com
- Vimeo.com

Titles and descriptions that get your video noticed.
The video you upload will have no information on it
that Google or other search engines can read. You
need to add a title and description to each video.

The titles are the same as you would use in your articles. Make sure you match the video title to a popular search word. I always add the city and state to the video title. For example "Flea Treatment Cleveland Ohio". That way, your video will nearly always show up when people do a local search.

You can also put your website's URL in the video description.

I also put complete addresses and phone numbers in video descriptions. This is mostly to help the search engines know that I'm local. Include popular search words and phrases when you can.

All of this helps the search engines find your video when a local search is made.

What Results You Will Get.

Although the methods discussed in this book work in every area, in any size business, there are differences in what you will get as results.

It all has to do with two factors; How many competitors you have in your local area, and if there is already someone using this kind of local online marketing.

LocalProfitGeyser.com

The number and quality of your competitors.
The larger the local area, and the more competitors you have, the harder it will be for your directory listings, articles, and videos to place high on the local search results. If you do a Google Maps search, and you get under 1,000 search results, it will be almost effortless to get a "Top Five" ranking in Google Plus Local. The more competition, the more important it is that your listings are complete. It becomes even more important that you have favorable customer reviews in your listing and it's also important that you are listed with the maximum number of online directories.

Someone else in your area is using this type of local online marketing.
This is very highly unlikely. If you Google your main search term for your industry, and one competitor of yours dominates the first page of Google with articles and video, you will end up sharing the first page with them. Again, this is highly unlikely. On a national basis, there may only be two or three people in your business even *aware* that this kind of marketing *exists*. And unless you share a city with them, their local online marketing will never affect you.

And even if they have the first page of Google dominated with articles, you can take away most of these positions with video and well written titles for the videos.

A look on Google in your area with the product you sell and your citywill assure you that you have no real competition.

It would be an incredibly unlikely event that you would be sharing Google page one with two other local people in your business. That means that two other business owners 1) read this book and 2) implemented what they learned in this book......that means your "local" area is so huge that you will make far more sales than most, even sharing the first page of a Google search.

When I do workshops, and if I have access to the attendee list, I'll get screenshots of the local searches for their product.
That means what their prospects would see if they did a local search.

I'll show the screenshots, changing them every second or so. I do this for every attendee. I do this to show that the prospect isn't listed well and they need to implement these ideas. In every case so far, I've never had an attendee that already had their information posted several times on the first page of a Google search.

You have no competition.

Your action plan.

Here is what I would do in the order that I would do it. If you are advanced, and have already taken care of some of this, skip to the items you need to take care of.

1) Go to Godaddy.com and register a domain name that has "what you do and your city and state" in the URL. The shorter, the better. Do not abbreviate the city and state.

"HTRdlrSFCA.com" is a terrible example and will never get you any good results. "HeaterDealerSanFrancisco.com" is much better. Google doesn't read some abbreviations and most people don't type them in.

2) Set up a hosting account. I use HostGator.com but GoDaddy has several inexpensive plans that will work just as well.

3) Go to Google and search for "Free website directories" You can do it or the person assembling your website can do it. Start submitting your website to website directories. This will get you free one way links to your website.

4) Go to www.ezinearticles.com and set up an account. Again, it's free. Follow their guidelines for writing an article. Be sure to pick a good category for the article to show up in. This is how search engines see your article by category. Write one 500-600 word article about an aspect of your business. Be sure to include your contact information and website in the author's box.

5) Buy a digital camera

6) Oh yeah, get a YouTube account. Again, this is free. Just go to www.YouTube.com to set up an account.

7) Add a few minute "Greeting Video" to your website. This is simply you saying "Hi" to the new person visiting your website. In the video you mention how you can help them, be sure to add your contact information. It helps a lot if you are actually in the video. It's also better if the video doesn't look professional. You want a friendly conversational video. It doesn't have to be more than a minute or two.

8) Add additional videos and articles as soon as possible.

9) Add your complete business profile to the local search directories listed in this book.

Very Important Message...

Now that you know how to generate *eager to buy customers* for your business, I have to tell you something very important; these component parts are a system. The online local directory listings, marketing website, articles, and videos, are inter-related.

I get calls from clients who have done this work themselves:

"Claude. I have a video on my website and nobody is coming in to buy anything"

After I ask a few questions, I find out that none of the videos were uploaded to any video hosting sites. The website wasn't submitted to any local search directories, and the website hasn't been mentioned in any articles.

Customers have to know you are in business. They have to actually *see* the videos before they can get excited about what's *in* the video.

This system does not work well at all if you only use the parts that you like. Every part adds to the effect of every other part.

I built a very strong, dominating, local online presence, by doing precisely what you have read in this book. But I have to point out; I did *everything* that was explained in this book to get great results. You have to follow all of the steps.

I recommend reading this book again with a yellow highlighter.

The 48 Ways To Improve Your Local Online Advertising and Marketing

Your written content:
1) Provide useful content to articles that search engines can find.

2) Use popular search words and phrases in the titles and content of the articles.

3) Use your city and state in the articles and in the "author's box" at the end of the articles.

4) Turn the search phrases into questions customers would ask, and make them your article titles.

5) Answer real questions customers ask in your articles. This will get them read.

6) Include your address and directions in your articles, or at least in your "author's box".

7) Do not talk about yourself in your articles. Make them instructional, not promotional.

8) Give useful information in your articles. The more detail, the better.

9) Write articles about products you sell or services you provide. Call them "Reviews".

10) Put the word "review" in the title if possible.

11) Send these articles to highly ranked article submission sites.

12) Change the title of the article, change the first paragraph, make changes to the wording of the rest of the article, change the wording of the "author's box" and send the article to different article sites. You'll get essentially the same article listed more than once this way.

13) Make sure the articles are about specific questions, or specific problems. This will make the readers feel the articles are just for them.

14) Put your website URL in the "author's box" You can put two links in the box if you have two websites. Do not put links in the article itself.

Your videos:

15) Read and record the articles to provide the audio for your videos.

16) Use a digital camera to record your videos.Most cameras are easy to use, can be recharged right from your computer, and contain editing software that will give you titles, credits, music, and the capability to submit your videos to YouTube.

17) Make sure the titles to your videos have the search words and search phrases in them so they will show up in a YouTube search. This will also make sure they show up in a Google search. Always put your city and state in the title of the video. This insures that they show up in a local Google search. Very important.

18) Make your videos short and less than 5 minutes. If the video is longer than ten minutes, break it up into part 1, part 2, etc. Give each video a separate set of links to your website and contact information.

19) Put your local business address in the description of the video and also put your website address.

20) Send your video to every high ranking video hosting site online.

21) When sending your videos to different sites, use different titles. This will cause more than one version to show up on a Google search.

22) Place these videos on your website. On the website, you can make the videos as long as you like. I wouldn't recommend more than 20 minutes though.

23) Make a "greetings" video, welcoming people to your website. Make it just a minute or two. You should be the one in the video. This starts a "relationship" with the customer.

24) Make sure you put your contact information, website address, and phone number in the videos themselves. Sometimes, when they are downloaded, the title and description on YouTube gets left behind. Your videos become viral this way.

25) Mention your city and address in the videos. Remember, these are local videos for local consumers. This will set you apart from the national merchants.

On Your Website:

26) Make your website URL the most popular search word or search phrase, and add your city and state to it, plus ".com"
This will get your website listed early in the local searches.

27) The title tag should be the first few most popular search words for your industry. This is how search engines find your website.

28) The description tag of your website should be a little less than 200 characters and be a complete sentence describing what is on your website. This is what will be in the search result, after the title.

29) Make the first paragraph or two on your website heavy with the first several most popular search phrases. This will help get the website ranked higher in local searches.

30) Put your articles on your website. List the article titles on the bottom of the first page. Put the articles themselves on their own page. Give each article its own page and own title tag.

31) At the end of each article, put a link to the first page of the website.

32) Be sure to put a complete "authors box" at the end of every article, even articles on your own website. That way, everything will show up in a local search, including your contact information.

33) Place your videos on the first page of your website. The first video should be your "Welcome" video.

34) Make sure all your business contact information is at the bottom of the first page of your website. A photo of you is a good idea too. That way the customer will see you as someone familiar.

35) Have descriptions of any photo or video placed under the photo or video. Any webmaster can do this. This text will help the search engine know what the video is about.

About your local search directory listings:

36) Make sure you submit the same information to every directory.

37) List the brands you sell, and describe each product category. When someone does a search by brand name, this will help your listing show up earlier.

38) Claim Your Listing! You must do this manually.

39) If possible, list your website greeting video in the videos allowed with your listing.

40) List your URL with your listing. Almost all directories will allow that.

41) Photos of your store or business will help consumers feel at ease when dealing with you.

42) Make sure your address and contact information is current. If you move and do not change your information; it may not show up for quite a while.

43) List any awards your business has won and any certifications you have earned. Remember to add anything else that provides credibility to your listing.

44) If you give credit terms, make sure you add that to your listing. List any credit cards you accept.

45) If you own more than one location, make sure each location has its own listing. Use separate phone numbers for each listing. Make sure the listings provide the city and state of that location.

46) If you have a voicemail box with an audio recording of your store greeting, or information you want customers to have, include this in your listings. I use www.voicenation.com

47) There are services that will submit your listing to nearly every online directory. But you must verify your listing information after it is posted. These services usually will not notify you when they post listings.

48) Again, Claim Your Business Listing.

"Sure, give a man a fish; you feed him for a day. Teach a man to fish; you feed him for a lifetime. But most people really just want a steady supply of fish"

-Claude Whitacre

Bonus Chapter;

Online VS Offline Local Advertising

Online marketing for local businesses is different from offline advertising (print, direct mail, radio, & TV).

In local online advertising, the customer is taking the first action. All online customers have shown an interest in your product or service category by going online and doing an online search. You are only getting people who are at least mildly interested.

You may be getting them at any point in the buying process. They may have had the first thought about your business for less than a minute before they went online for information.

They may look for your information when they are in the research stage, at the decision stage, or when they are ready to buy. And you have information online that will help them move forward at any stage of the buying process.

The information you post online has a long life. Your articles, videos, and local search directory listings will be there (assuming you renew your listings) for a long time.

So the customer can get information at their own pace. The customer can go back online anytime and read the same content, see the same videos, or visit your website.

One big advantage you will have, if you use the ideas in this book, is that an initial online search for information will result in seeing your content, your listing, your video, far more often than your nearest competitor. You can literally crowd the competition out of the first page Google search results.

Another major difference between online and offline advertising and marketing is that online advertising, the way we showed you in this book, is practically free. There is just some initial labor involved.

With offline advertising, the prospect is not looking for you or what you sell. You are virtually interrupting them with your ads. When people are reading a magazine, they are not looking for your advertisement. They are looking either for enjoyment or information.

Offline advertisements work in two ways. "Image" ads create a good feeling in the prospect's mind when they think of your brand. When most people think of advertising, they think of this kind of ad. These ads take many repetitions to create any effect. The main benefit is that they either support a field sales force, or they support local sales advertising. These ads do not generate phone calls or sales. In local small business this isn't the way to go.

The other kind of advertising is a direct response advertisement. These ads create desire for the product, give reasons to buy it, give reasons to buy it from *you*, and give reasons to buy it *now*. These ads can create an immediate profit and will also create the brand recognition of the image ads.

The reason advertisers avoid this type of ad is that these ads are more complicated. There is more to the ad and you will be able to tell within a day or two after the ad runs, if it worked. Most small business owners can't stand the knowledge that their ads aren't working. So they stick to ads that "get their name out there", without a tangible result.

Offline advertising helps your online advertising. Online advertising has little effect on your offline advertising.

In every print ad we run (at our local store) we include the website address. This gives the customer something to see that takes them away from any competitive ads. This also allows a print ad to include all the articles, and especially videos on your website.

Of course, your website acts as an expanded advertisement and advice source that leads the customer to your business.

The reverse does not happen. It's very difficult to lead your online prospect to an offline advertisement. You would never say on your website "Be sure to look for my ad in the newspaper". And why would you want to? The best information and marketing tools you have are online. The space is almost free, and it's unlimited.

Then why should you still advertise offline with traditional methods like TV, radio, newspapers, and direct mail? Several reasons actually;

1) Some people either do not have a computer, or they never do a search online. Some use their computer only for games, only as a word processor, or only to get and send e-mail.

2) Sometimes the interest in your product isn't enough to cause an online search, but a print advertisement (or radio-TV), may get the customer thinking about buying.

3) Some people are ready to buy at the moment they see your ad offline. This can cause them to go buy from *you* rather than from someone else. This is the main reason I continue my advertising offline. Mostly I use direct mail.

In America, the sharp increases in local internet searches are killing two of the main ways to advertise offline locally; Newspapers and the Yellow Pages.

This is important. If you are currently advertising in your local newspaper or in your local Yellow Pages, and you have evidence (real sales results, not just buzz from the ad rep) that the ads are creating an immediate profit, please do not stop advertising this way.

In no way am I saying you shouldn't advertise in your newspaper or in the Yellow Pages. My only purpose here is to make your business more profitable. Never stop doing something that creates a profit.

The year 2010 is the first year that our online marketing generated more profit than our offline advertising. But I would never think of stopping my direct mail offers until they stopped generating a profit. Plus, these ads drive people to my local website.

I can only tell you what happened for me with my method of online advertising;
My business had a sharp rise over three months...and never went back down.

Whether you want to do the work yourself, or would like us to do everything for you...I wish you every success. Please e-mail your results to me. I love success stories.

claude@localprofitgeyser.com

Special Section:
If You Own A Company That Sells To Independent Business Owners

Do your customers resell to end consumers? If so, I can create a permanent online marketing pipeline that will benefit both you and your customers.

Do you provide your resellers with advertisements to use locally, and maybe even help with the advertising cost to promote your products or service?

I have an idea that can help you market your products in every local area that you have dealers. Your dealers would get new customers at little cost to them, and you would increase sales dramatically at *no* cost to you.

Do I have your attention?

Here is a problem with every local advertisement your dealer network runs:

The paid advertisement dies a quick death.

Print, direct mail, newspaper, radio or TV...it doesn't matter. After the advertisement is paid for and runs, the effect lasts a few days at most and then is gone...until the *next* ad is paid for.

When you provide useful content about your products and services online, this attracts *buyers* even more than any advertising you could do. And an amazing thing happens to good online content.... It doesn't disappear. In fact it grows. An article or video that has real helpful information in it gets passed around to different websites and goes viral.

If you write an article that gets posted online, a year from now, more people will be reading it every day than are reading it today. And you never pay another dime for the exposure.

Another problem:

Print and broadcast advertising only attracts people at the end of the buying process. It ignores the other 95% of buyers that are still in the information gathering stage.

There is only one place that people can go to get information at every stage of the buying process. That's *online*.

Highly informative articles and video are what attracts online shoppers to your brand, your products, and your dealers.

Another problem with print and broadcast advertising:

Every time the print or broadcast ad runs, win or lose, you have to pay for it again...and again...forever.

Local online advertising is virtually free, if you do it yourself. And it is far more effective than offline advertising. Two thirds of all local shopping starts online. Your dealers need to *be there*. And because articles and videos go viral, there are more people seeing your ad online a year after you run it than there are the first day.

Here is how you can help your dealers and yourself:

Host a "Local Online Marketing" seminar for your customers. In 3 hours they will learn everything they could possibly need to know to promote *your* products online....driving eager buyers into *their* business to buy *your* offering.

Your customers will learn;
1) How to dominate their local search engines with searches for your product category.
2) How to use articles and video to create a heated desire in the consumer's mind to buy your product from them.
3) How to build a website that is a marketing magnet; bringing in buyers for your product.

Your customers will see this extra effort as a real benefit to buying through you. You are helping them with *their* business, not just selling them product.

That is truly "going the extra mile" for your customers.

Are your dealers going into the internet marketing age kicking and screaming?

I'll show you how to help your dealers painlessly use local online marketing to sell your product. There is no obligation and your dealers will love you for providing them with the latest, and most profitable, competitive advantage.

And the best news? In most instances....
You will get the entire program delivered for *free*.

You can find out more at www.claudewhitacre.com

"It's not who you are. It's what you do that defines you"

-Batman

Shameless Promotional Section:

How to profit from what you've learned

You now know everything you need to know to create tons of highly qualified local traffic to your website and your place of business. I sincerely hope you use this information so you can get results like I have, and like my clients have. Like I said at the beginning, you have three options.

Your Options:

Do nothing.
Continue to blame the economy, the weather, the government, or the stars for your business problems. Most of these people won't even make it to the end of this book. Too much trouble. Just by reading this book, you have shown you are probably not in this group.

Do everything yourself.
This book is written to provide you with every trick, technique, strategy, and resource you need to get phenomenal results from your effort. If you choose this route, and carry through with it... I applaud you. Work ethic is something I admire.

Let us do everything for you.
In the paragraph below you'll get a description of what we can do for you.

If we do everything for you:

We *still* need a few things from you...

1) 30-40 minutes in a telephone interview where we get answers to questions customers might ask. This is after you fill out the application and questionnaire. This will be recorded, and parts may be used to create the audio for videos.

2) A complete application and questionnaire. This will let us know about your business, area you are in, and how to get the best results for you. We will also need this very information to submit your business profile to every local search directory. This application process may even take an hour or so.

If we think this is a good fit, we will call you. At that time we will answer any remaining questions and arrange for payment. Since I cannot ever change a fee when it is in print, just go to www.LocalProfitGeyser.com and click on "Fees". We will not charge you, or even accept payment, until after we talk to you on the phone.

We only accept one business in each zip code per business category. The first one in... wins.

That's it. We take care of everything else.

Now here is a nearly complete list of what we do for you:

1) We choose the best website name (with your provided information) for a local search.

2) We do a "keyword search" to find the best search words and phrases to use in your website URL, your website content, your search listing descriptions, and your articles and videos.

3) We create a marketing website. If you want us to use your logos, we will. If you want us to use headings, a certain font style, or photos from your existing website, we will.

4) We create a Frequently Asked Questions page for your new website. If you already have one, we'll use parts of it, all of it, or add to it. This page will become powerful text for the search engines to "crawl". This will also lead your readers to come into your store. This website is designed to do one thing only; bring buyers into your business.

5) We interview you by telephone for 45 minutes to an hour to get information on your business. The call is recorded. This audio is used to create articles, video, and other content.

6) We create three articles from your interview. We may call you to add a fact or clarify a point. (E-mail is OK too. You specify). These are keyword rich articles designed to get read, and are written for the reader to want *more*. These articles will have links to your new website. Your local contact information is included with each article to make sure they show up in a local online search.

7) We video and edit your business greeting video and place it on your new website.
If you have a video of yourself, we may use it. Otherwise, we create the video from pictures and the audio from our interview with you.

8) We create and edit 10 videos from your interview and place them on your new website. We then submit your videos to 50 different video submission sites.

9) We create a business profile about your business to submit to search directories and Yellow Page directories. We place your Business profile on 200 local search and Yellow Page directories.

10) We submit your new website to all the major search engines

11) **As a Special Bonus**, we'll rewrite your articles, by hand, at least ten times each. Each article will have a unique Keyword rich headline, and the content will be rewritten to be easily read. We then submit each of these articles to 1,030 article submission sites, and also place them on your new website, in pages behind the front page. This will create hundreds of links to your website, and hundreds of articles magnetically attracting buyers to your business.

We can teach you how to fish.... or we can just keep delivering buckets of fish.

Our Guarantee

We guarantee at least 200 links back to your new website within 90 days. We also guarantee at least one local Google "Top Ten" organic listing generated by us. If you do not get at least one listing (you should get several) we will continue to work for you, at no additional cost, creating valuable content, until you get at least one "Top Ten" organic listing on a local Google search.

Only one identical business per zip code.No exceptions. Contact us to see if your zip code is available for your business category.

"But Claude! I already have a website. My webmaster can do SEO. Do I really need this?"

Local Profit Geyser is *not* an SEO service. We build a new website for you. We do not work on any existing website.

SEO (Search Engine Optimization) experts are really good at getting your website listed highly in the search engines. That's an admirable goal.

But even the best SEO service can only get your website listed *once* in a local search. Having your website highly listed is not nearly as profitable as listing highly *desirable* information or videos that buyers *seek out before they buy or want to see.*

And with Local Profit Geyser, your goal isn't *one* high ranking listing of your website. With Local Profit Geyser, your goal (and mine) is multiple listings on the first page of a local Google search.

With Local Profit Geyser, you don't get just one listing... you get dozens of highly effective marketing pieces that will easily get listed in Google.

If you already have an SEO expert, great. That has nothing to do with what we do for you. And he/she can work on your website all they want. The higher they get that one website listing to rank, the better for you.

But that has nothing to do with the services we provide.

Special Offer For Readers Of This Book

I recently did a three hour workshop on the nuts and bolts of Local Online Marketing. Half of the time was invested in instruction and half of the time was answering specific questions from the audience. For most of the people in the audience, this was a Game Changer.

In my speeches, I make an offer for the entire three hour event, including workbook, CDs, and DVDs of the workshop for $997. This offer includes some telephone consulting time.

As a reader of this book, I'm willing to make the entire program digitally downloadable for just $97.*This offer does NOT include telephone consulting time.*

Simply go to **www.localprofitgeyserseminar.com/bookoffer** to get all the details on how you can get the entire program for a measly $97. Nobody gets that website address except readers of this book. This is a marketing test.

If you do not see this offer on the website, it's because I discontinued the offer.

My sincere wish is that you profit greatly from the information you received in this book. Please e-mail your success story to claude@localprofitgeyser.com

Recommended reading;

Get Found Now by Richard Geasey and Shannon Evans. This is one of a dozen books I bought when I was learning about local online marketing. They almost all cover the exact same thing, getting listed in local search directories. I chose this book because it shows you exactly the steps on filling out the forms to submit your listing to most of the major local search directories. The explanations are clear, and the book price is low.

The Unfair Advantage Small Business Advertising Manual. I wrote it. If you want to know how to advertise your small business offline to get the most profit from each ad...this is the book.

Everything Dan Kennedy writes. He teaches nothing about online marketing. But if you want to know how to know anything about offline marketing, this is the guy. And just about everything in marketing offline has an application when selling online.

Influence by Robert Cialdini. The most powerful book on using persuasion to sell anything ever written. If you want to know what motivates people to buy, this is the book.

Local Online Advertising For Dummies by Court Cunningham and Stephanie Brown.
I cannot recommend this book highly enough. It has a few things that are in my book, and just about everything that isn't. The book is promotional in spots, but it's a treasure trove of information about local marketing online.

The Ultimate Sales Machine by Chet Holmes. This is not a book on online marketing. It is a book about how to use information marketing in the offline world. There are also chapters on hiring the perfect employee. There are several techniques in the book that I have used successfully to market this book, and market my speaking services. If you want to sell your product in huge quantities, this is the book.

All these books can be ordered from Amazon.com. My advertising book can be ordered either from Amazon.com or from my website at: www.claudewhitacre.com. There are some extra bonuses if you order from my website.

Additional Recommended Books:

The Ultimate Guide To Building and Marketing Your Online Business With Free Tools
By Gabriela Taylor

From Local To Global: Taking Your Business To New Markets
By Gabriela Taylor

SEO Made Simple (Second Edition): Strategies For Domination The World's Largest Search Engine
By Michael H. Fleischner

Internet Marketing for Small Business Owners: 10 Internet Marketing Steps to Making More Money and Dominating Your Competitors Online
By James Dreesen and Travis Van Slooten

The Handmade Marketplace: How to Sell Your Crafts Locally, Globally, and On-Line
By Kari Chapin

Glenn J Fournier's Marketing Secrets for Small Business: No-Nonsense Guide To Marketing Your Business Online
By Glenn J Fournier

The Laptop Millionaire: How Anyone Can Escape the 9 to 5 and Make Money Online
By Mark Anastasi

Simple Online Reputation Management For Your Local Business
By Jack Mize

Nathan Big's Ultimate Online Marketing Guide: How ToTakeover Your Market, Triple Your Business And Finally Live The Good Life
By Nathan Big

Jason Davidson's Guide to Marketing Your Local Business Online: Your Complete Guide to Local Online Marketing Success
By Jason Davidson

Internet Marketing for Dummies
By Frank Catalano and Bud E. Smith

Local Search Marketing for Business: A How-To Guide
By Sarah Moraes, Michael Schwarts, Elise Redlin-Cook, and David Gould

Cat O'Donnell's Guide to Marketing Your Business Online in San Antonio: Lessons in online marketing for local businesses
By Catherine O'Donnell

Complete Local Business Online Marketing Strategies Revealed:: How to Double (Or Better!) Your Customer Base
By Melanie Pascal and Stephane Pascal

Kendall Beleshko's Guide to Dominating Local Online Marketing: Your Customers Are Looking for You Online... Can They Find You?
By Kendall Beleshko

Can Your Customers Find You Online?: A How-To Guide to Marketing Your Local Small Business Online
By Charisa Jones Pruitt

Eva Szakal's No-Nonsense Guide to An Unstoppable Stream Of Local Customers: Explode Growth & Boost Profits through Effective Online Marketing
By Eva Szakal

Chris Ripley's Online Marketing 101: No-Nonsense Guide To Marketing Your Business Online
By Chris Ripley

Local Business Insane Results: How local businesses are cashing in on marketing their businesses online
By Mr Jason C.

Marketing Your Local Business Online: Key Strategies to Increasing Sales and Profit Using the Internet
By Sherry Han and Daisy Huang

Damon Blythe's Guide to Marketing Your Business Online: Your Customers Are Looking for You Online… Can They Find You?
By Damon Blythe

Ultimate Guide to Building Your Business Online: Fastest Way Ever To Get Results, Get Customers and Crush Your Competition
By Chuck Choate

Engagement Marketing: How Small Business Wins in a Socially Connected World
By Gail F. Goodman

About The Author

Claude Whitacre is the author of the book **The Unfair Advantage Small Business Advertising Manual**. Claude owns a successful retail store, The Sweeper Store in Wooster, Ohio with his wife Cheryl. He uses the exact same online marketing methods to promote his retail business as he teaches in this book.

This retail store has provided a lab to test marketing and advertising ideas for the past twelve years. (At the time of this writing) Claude owns www.LocalProfitGeyser.com which offers a complete service for business owners to promote locally, driving ready buyers into their brick and mortar business or to the phone ready to buy. Claude divides his time between running his businesses, and speaking to groups of business owners about local online marketing and offline advertising strategies.

Claude and his wife Cheryl live quietly in the small college town of Wooster Ohio.

You can learn more about how Claude can help you at www.claudewhitacre.com

www.ingramcontent.com/pod-product-compliance
Lightning Source LLC
Chambersburg PA
CBHW051532170526
45165CB00002B/698